*Wildflowers Along
Forest and Mesa Trails*

Wildflowers Along Forest and Mesa Trails

Nelson T. Bernard

Illustrations by Dan Godfrey

UNIVERSITY OF NEW MEXICO PRESS

Albuquerque

Library of Congress Cataloging in Publication Data

Bernard, Nelson T., 1925–
    Wildflowers along forests and mesa trails.

    Bibliography: p.
    Includes index.
    1. Wild flowers—New Mexico—Albuquerque Region—
Identification.   I. Godfrey, Dan, 1934–   .   II. Title.
QK176.B47   1984   582.13'09789'61   83-23344
ISBN 0-8263-0730-2

Contents

Preface

This book introduces you to only a few of the more common flowering plants that grow wild in the Southwest. They may be found in empty lots and along sidewalks. You may find them in your backyard, in fields, woods, arroyos, and along roads. As spring blends into summer, flowering plants follow the warmer days up the mountainside. The season for outdoor activities coincides with the time of year when plants bloom. Plant watching, like people watching or bird watching, is an exercise in observing the endless variety and uniqueness offered by nature. This book is intended to guide plant watchers in conjunction with other activities. Plant watching should provide an interesting interlude during excursions around town, along the river, or into the nearby mountains.

To save botanical confusion, scientific names in Latin are used to identify plants around the world. In this book both the common names and the Latin name have been used. Many plants have several common names. You may know a plant as a scarlet gilia while someone else may call it a skyrocket. You both are correct. I have listed as many common names as I am aware of for each plant, and all these names appear in the index, along with the Latin names.

In keeping with the use of common names, as few technical terms have been used as possible. A glossary defines those that are used in the text, and explanations of these terms are usually included in the text as well. Some general illustrations at the beginning of the book clarify plant anatomy and its terminology.

The book is arranged as simply as possible, to make it easy to use. Part 1 lists several poisonous plants, ranging from those that are deadly to poison ivy. Parts 2, 3, and 4 group plants in general categories that are easy to spot: the distinctive cacti and yuccas are grouped together (part 2), as are several vines and other creeping and climbing plants (part 3) and trees, shrubs, and bushes (part 4). Some plants are categorized as bushes even though they do not always grow in enormous clumps. As a common-sense guide, this book describes the majority of plants but there are some exceptions to most descriptions of size, shape, and color.

Part 5 includes a variety of plants, broken down by color descriptions. Here again remember that colors come in many shades and variations. If you are trying to pin down the name of a plant that looks blue to you,

you may find it here classified as a purple plant. Most blossoms come in ranges of color.

In addition to listing identifying features of the plants, I have included some ethnobotany (studies of the use of plants)—information on poisonous plants, those with medicinal values, edible ones, and so on.

The plants noted as poisonous ususally cause skin rashes, upset stomachs, or diarrhea. However, there are some that are fatal if eaten (water hemlock, for example). Unless you are positive about the identification of any plant, play it safe and do not put it into your mouth.

Plant distribution is dependent upon elevation, direction and steepness of slopes, sunlight and shade, day and night temperatures, soil, and surfacial geology. However, the most important factor in this hot, arid Southwest is moisture—rain and snowfall. As elevation increases, so does precipitation. Albuquerque averages 20 cm (8 in) annually while on top of Sandia Crest, just a few miles away, the average is approximately 90 cm (35 in). As the altitude increases, the temperature decreases. Therefore, plants requiring cooler, more moist sites may be found higher on the mountain slopes.

The Anatomy of
a Plant

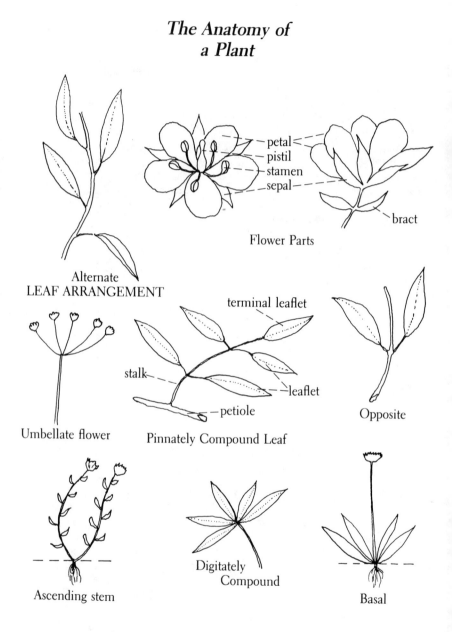

Flower Parts

petal
pistil
stamen
sepal
bract

Alternate
LEAF ARRANGEMENT

terminal leaflet

stalk

leaflet

petiole

Opposite

Umbellate flower

Pinnately Compound Leaf

Ascending stem

Digitately
Compound

Basal

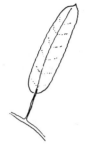

Linear

Lanceolate

Palmate Compound

Palmate

Cactus Areole

lobe

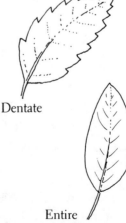

Dentate

Serrate

Entire
(smooth)

Glossary

Alternate	Leaves arranged first on one side, then on the other, at different levels on the stem. Not opposite one another.
Areole	Grouping of cactus spines.
Bilabiate	Two-lipped
Bract	Reduced or modified leaf at base of flower stalk.
Calyx	Outer envelope of flower, usually green.
Compound	Composed of leaflets.
Deciduous	Losing leaves in winter.
Dentate	Toothed.
Digitate	Resembling fingers. This adjective is used to describe compound leaves consisting of leaflets clustered at the apex of leaf stalk like fingers of a hand.
Foliage	Ordinary, well developed leaves.
Herbaceous	Having little or no woody texture; often green in color.
Keel	A projection resembling the keel or main timber of a boat.
Lanceolate	Narrow, tapering to the apex.
Leaflet	A division of a compound leaf.
Linear	Long and of a nearly uniform, narrow width (used to describe leaves).
Lobe	A rounded projection of a leaf.
Nerve	An unbranched leaf vein.
Opposite	Across from one another, as leaves on a stem.
Ovate	Egg-shaped.
Pad	Segment of pricklypear cactus.
Palmate	Having lobes radiating from base, like fingers on hand.

Perennial	Living for an indefinite number of years.
Petal	A segment of the inner envelope of a flower, usually the colored portion.
Petiole	Foot of leaf stalk.
Pistil	Female organ of flower.
Pubescence	Hairiness, on leaves, stems, or stalks.
Raceme	An unbranched, elongated grouping of flowers.
Rhizome	A prostrate stem on or just below ground surface.
Rib	A primary vein, especially when prominent.
Rootstalk	*See rhizome.*
Segment	Part of a compound leaf or other organ.
Sepal	One segment of the outer envelope of flower.
Spine	Sharp pointed woody structure; thorn.
Stalk	Stem on which a leaf, flower, or other organ is attached.
Stamen	Male or pollen-producing organ.
Stem	The axis or portion of a plant above the root on which the leaves and flowers are borne.
Taproot	Primary root.
Terminal	Growing at the end of a stem; a growth at the end of a stem.
Trifoliate	Having three leaves or leaflets.
Tubular	Tube-like.
Umbellate	More or less flat topped with all flower stalks arising from the same point, like the ribs of an umbrella.
Undulate	Wavy.
Vein	A strand of vascular tissue in a leaf, especially if branched. An unbranched strand of vascular tissue is a *nerve*.
Wing	A thin, expanded extension of a seed or fruit.

Selected references

Arnberger, Leslie P. *Flowers of the Southwest Mountains.* 4th Ed. Globe, Ariz.: Southwest Parks and Monument Association, 1968.

Benson, Lyman. *The Cacti of Arizona.* 3d. Ed. Tucson: University of Arizona Press, 1969.

Coulter, John M., and Nelson, Aven. *New Manual of Rocky Mountain Botany.* New York: American Book Company, 1909.

Dodge, Natt N. *100 Roadside Wildflowers of Southwest Uplands.* Globe, Ariz.: Southwest Parks and Monument Association, 1967.

Elias, Thomas S., and Dykeman, Peter A. *Field Guide to North American Edible Wild Plants.* New York: Outdoor Life Books, 1982.

Elmore, Francis H. *Shrubs and Trees of the Southwest Uplands.* Globe, Ariz.: Southwest Parks and Monument Association, 1976.

Harrington, H. D. *Edible Native Plants of the Rocky Mountains.* Albuquerque: University of New Mexico Press, 1967.

Kearney, Thomas H., and Peebles, Robert H. *Arizona Flora.* Berkeley and Los Angeles: University of California Press, 1960.

Krochmal, Arnold, Walters, Russell S., and Doughty, Richard M. *A Guide to Medicinal Plants of Appalachia.* Agriculture Handbook No. 400. Washington, D.C.: U.S. Government Printing Office, 1969.

Little, Elbert L. Jr. *Southwestern Trees.* Agriculture Handbook No. 9. Washington, D.C.: U.S. Government Printing Office, 1950.

Patraw, Pauline M. *Flowers of the Southwest Mesas.* Globe, Ariz.: Southwest Parks and Monument Association, 1951.

U.S. Forest Service. *Range Plant Handbook.* Washington, D.C.: U.S. Government Printing Office, 1937.

Wyeth Laboratories. *The Sinister Garden.* Philadelphia, Penna.: Wyeth Laboratories, 1966.

1

Poisonous Plants

WATER HEMLOCK
Cicuta Douglasii

Other names: Poison water hemlock, western water hemlock, Douglas water hemlock.

Flower: White; July and August.

Description: Water hemlock may reach 120 cm (4 ft) in height with an umbellate cluster (more or less flat-topped with all stalks arising from the same point) of white flowers at the extremities of the stems. These flowers of this poisonous plant are similar to those of carrots, dill, and cowparsnips, which are edible. Water hemlock has been fatally mistaken for these plants.

Where found: This plant is found throughout New Mexico in wet places and along ditches and streams from 1892 m (6,000 ft) to 2744 m (9,000 ft) in elevation.

Water hemlock has gained the reputation of being the most violently poisonous plant to warm-blooded animals, including humans, in the North Temperate Zone. The poison, cicutoxin, a violent convulsant, acts directly on the central nervous system. Symptoms may appear within 15 minutes after ingestion. The first indication of water hemlock poisoning is excessive salivation, quickly followed by tremors and spasmodic convulsions interspersed with periods of relaxation. The convulsions are extremely violent with evidence of abdominal pains. Death may occur within 15 minutes after the symptoms first appear and comes from respiratory failure following a period of complete paralysis.

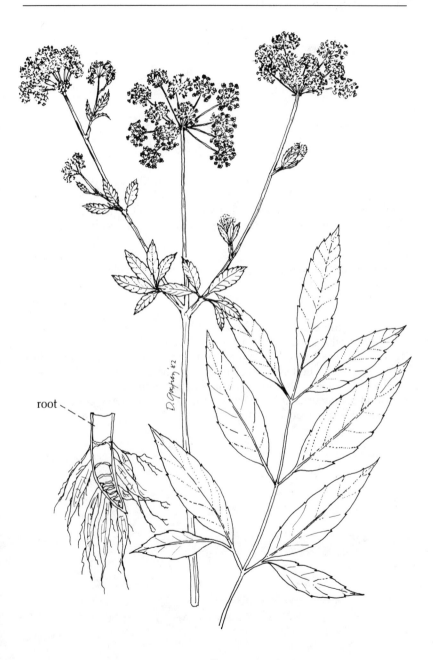

root

POISON IVY
Rhus radicans

Other names: Mala, poison vine, poison oak.

Flower: Yellowish-white to greenish-white: April to September.

Description: Poison ivy can be either a low shrub or a woody vine that grows on trees or shrubs. The lusterless, oak-like leaves are trifoliate (with three leaflets); the middle leaflet has a longer stalk. The fruit is yellowish-white, shiny, and usually without hairs. Poison ivy is deciduous (loses its leaves in winter).

Where found: Poison ivy is found in rich soils in shady areas of arroyos and canyons up to 2,439 m (8,000 ft) in elevation. It proliferates quickly on disturbed or overused areas such as those near public picnic grounds.

All parts of the plant should be avoided since they contain urushiol, a nonvolatile oil that may cause painful swelling and eruptions of the skin. Toxin-laden smoke from burning poison ivy plants can cause the same severe reaction. The best remedy in case of contact is to wash to exposed areas immediately with a strong soap. Clothes worn while exposed should be laundered as urushiol remains on them as can later reinfect the wearer. In cases of severe reaction, consult a doctor.

NIGHTSHADE
Solanum elaeagnifolium

Other names: Silverleaf nightshade, bull nettle, horse nettle, trompillo.

Flower: Violet or blue; May to October.

Description: Nightshade is a perennial plant 30 cm (1 ft) to 1 m (3 ft) tall with white-hairy leaves and stems. The stems and leaf ribs have short, stiff spines. The flower petals extend backward with yellow stamens projecting to the front. Berries are orange or yellow.

Where found: Nightshade grows in open woods and disturbed soils from the lower foothills up to 1,829 m (6,000 ft) in elevation. In town, it is found along arroyos, empty lots, and between sidewalks and curbs.

Nightshade, a troublesome weed in cultivated fields and home gardens, is difficult to eradicate. The leaves and unripe berries of this plant contain solamine, a substance that is poisonous to humans if ingested. However, it is reported that the Pima Indians add the crushed fruits of the nightshade to milk when making cheese.

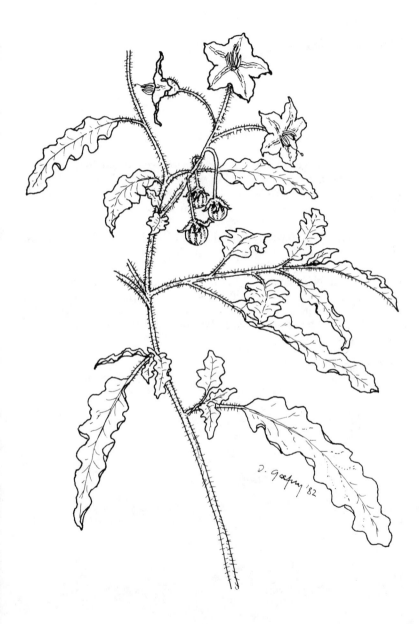

JIMSON WEED
Datura meteloides

Other names: Sacred datura, datura, thornapple, tolguache, Indian apple, moon lily.

Flower: White, sometimes tinged with lavender; May to October.

Description: A large, coarse, gray-green plant that grows in low, spreading clumps. The unpleasant smelling leaves are large with slightly undulating edges and a velvety underside. The large, fragrant flowers are conspicuous, funnel-shaped, and grow individually from a fork in the stem.

Where found: Jimson weed is found along roadsides, arroyos, empty lots, and disturbed areas up to about 1,982 m (6,500 ft) in elevation.

All parts of the plant contain the drug atropine, a poison that may cause death if ingested. California Indians mashed all parts of the plant into a liquid or dried it into a powder and used these for religious purposes. They also made a decoction from all parts of the plant and used it as a disinfectant or sometimes to deaden pain.

LOCOWEED
Astragalus missouriensis

Other names: Milkvetch, rattleweed, loco, poison vetch.

Flower: Purplish, but occasionally may be white; April and May.

Description: Locoweed is a short, herbaceous plant that seldom grows more than 15 cm (6 in) tall. The entire plant is pubescent (covered by small hairs). The leaves are pinnately compound (leaflets arranged along the leaf stalk). The bottom petals are usually arched or bent. The mottled reddish-brown seed pods are papery.

Where found: This plant is found in areas up to 2,134 m (7,000 ft) in elevation where other plant cover has been disturbed and along roads.

The only way to identify this plant is by the mature seed. There are many species of astragalus, and some are good forage plants. Others, however, absorb selenium from the soil and become poisonous to livestock, especially horses, who are afflicted with loco disease (from the Spanish word for *crazy*) when they eat too much locoweed. This disease is usually characterized by general sluggishness and inactivity, impaired vision, and varying degrees of paralysis in the hind legs.

ground line

PASQUEFLOWER
Pulsatilla ludoviciana

Other names: Windflower, wild crocus.

Flower: Purplish outside, either purplish or yellowish inside; spring.

Description: Pasqueflower stems are usually leafless and are normally less than 30 cm (1 ft) tall. Stems have silky hairs. The leaves are usually at the base of the plant or just below the flower. Each leaf is divided several times into narrow, lance-shaped lobes. Up to 3 flowers grow at the end of the stem, each with 5 to 8 petal-like sepals. The entire plant is hairy.

Where found: Pasqueflower grows on nearly dry to moist soils in sunny locations from 1,220 m (4,000 ft) to 3,049 (10,000 ft) in elevation. In this area they are found near the Pineflat picnic area on New Mexico 14.

Some Indians have made poultices from crushed pasqueflower leaves as a treatment for rheumatism. However, a poultice can blister the skin if left on too long. The plants contain a violent irritant, the drug pulsatilla, and if taken internally may cause vomiting and purging accompanied by pain, tremors, and eventual collapse. It is best to leave this plant alone.

ground line

DEATH CAMAS
Zigadenus elegans

Other names: Mountain death camas, wand lily.

Flower: Yellowish-white; July and August.

Description: Death camas grows from a bulb. It has a smooth leafless flower stem reaching 60 cm (24 in) in height. The narrow grasslike leaves grow from the base of the plant. Flowers consist of six egg-shaped petals blooming on a single, unbranched stem.

Where found: This plant is usually found in the rich soils of the moist, cool sites of coniferous forests from 1,524 m (5,000 ft) to 3,049 m (10,000 ft) in elevation.

All parts of the death camas plants are poisonous. Its bulb is similar to a wild onion, and the two are frequently confused. One way to distinguish between them is to crush the leaves. If there is no onion odor, do not eat the plant.

IRIS
Iris missouriensis

Other names: Flag, Rocky Mountain iris, western blue flag, fleur de lis.

Flower: Pale blue to purple, fading to white with age; May to September.

Description: This perennial plant is similar to the garden variety. Grass-like, the leaves are about 2.5 cm (1 in) wide. The flowering stem is produced from the root stalk and two or more blossoms may appear on the stem.

Where found: This iris is found throughout the mountains in the meadows, open parks, and along roads up to 2,896 m (9,500 ft) in elevation.

Irises are the most common plants in the home flower gardens. The iris has been bred to produce beautiful blossoms. The rootstalk of the iris is reportedly poisonous and should not be eaten.

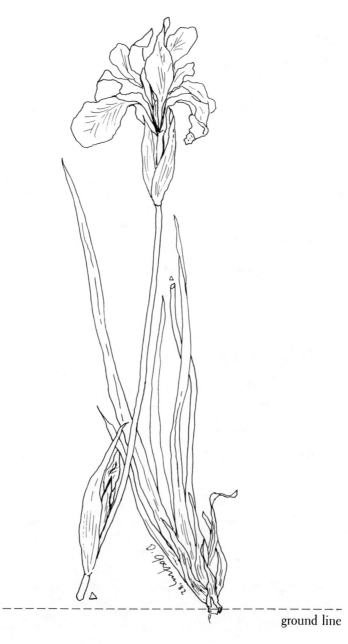

ground line

LARKSPUR
Delphenium Barbeyi

Other names: Barbey larkspur, subalpine larkspur, espuela del caballero.

Flower: Dark blue to purple; July and August.

Description: The stems of this plant normally grow 1 m (3 ft) or more in height but may reach 2 m (6 ft). The leafy, stout stems are hollow, dark green, and hairy. Leaves have stalks and grow alternately on the stem. Deep clefts divide the leaf into 5 segments, each of which is cleft in turn. Flowers grow in short, dense clusters on narrow-bracted, ascending, sticky-hairy stems.

Where found: Larkspur is found in the heavy dampish soils of ravines and meadows in subalpine forests up to 3,658 m (12,000 ft) in elevation. It can also be found on the high slopes of the Sandia and Manzano mountains, especially above Capulin Spring in the Sandias.

The name *larkspur* is descriptive of the backward projecting spur that resembles the rear spur of birds. Larkspurs are poisonous when ingested.

2

Cacti and Yuccas

CANE CHOLLA
Opuntia imbricata

Other names: Cane cactus, candelabrum, walkingstick cholla.

Flower: Magenta to yellow-bronze; June to July.

Description: An erect, many-branched, cylindrical-stemmed cactus reaching 2 m (6 ft) in height. The flowers are 5 cm (2 in) to 8 cm (3 in) across. The spines are reddish-brown and the fruit, often mistaken for the flower, is dry and yellow.

Where found: Cane cholla is usually found in association with grasslands on the mesas and foothills up to 2,287 m (7,500 ft) in elevation. It is prevalent along the western and northern edge of the Sandia Mountains and along the roads to Santa Fe and the Jemez Mountains.

The external woody structure of cane cholla is filled with a spongy mass that enables it to absorb water rapidly and to store it for use in time of drought. When the plant dies, the spongy material decomposes, leaving a hollow woody frame filled with diamond-shaped holes. It is this woody skeleton that is used to make picture frames, walkingsticks, lamps, and curios. The cholla skeleton is a favorite habitat of the scorpion, so it is advisable to kick the wood thoroughly before handling it.

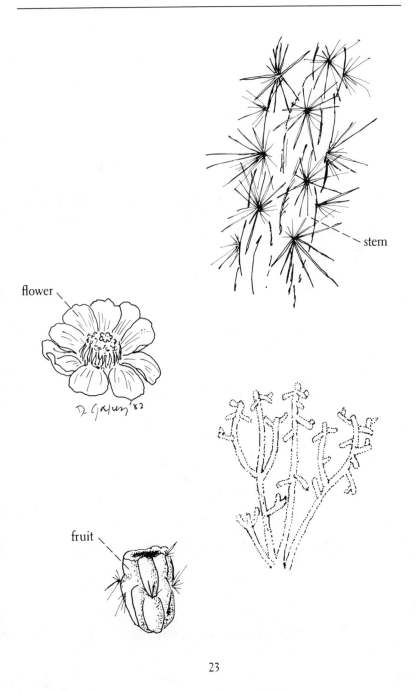

stem

flower

D. Gaken '82

fruit

CLUB CHOLLA
Opuntia clavata

Other names: Foot dagger, clump cholla, dagger thorn cholla.

Flower: Yellow; summer.

Description: A mat-forming cholla usually not more than 7 cm (3 in) to 10 cm (4 in) high and about 1–2 (3–6 ft) in diameter. Its spines are ashy-gray, longitudinally ridged and grooved, and grow near the upper part of the joint. The largest spine in each group is dagger-like. The flower is 3 cm (1¼ in) to 5 cm (2 in) across.

Where found: The club cholla is found in sandy soils of the valleys and grassy slopes and in the foothills up to 2,439 m (8,000 ft) in elevation.

Club cholla is usually hidden by other plants. As a result, many unwary hikers have been injured by this short cactus with spines stiff and sharp enough to penetrate leather shoes.

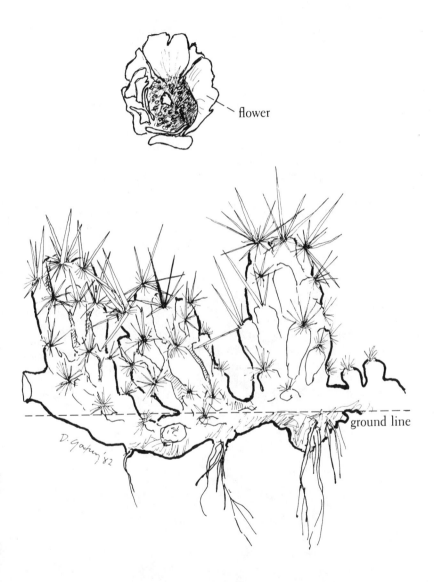

flower

ground line

D. Gafney '82

PRICKLYPEAR
Opuntia macrorhiza

Other names: Tuna, Indian fig.

Flower: Yellow when fresh, but in the afternoon it may change to shades of red and orange as it wilts; May and June.

Description: This plant grows in a spreading clump and has flat segments (pads) with areoles (bunches) of needles primarily along the edges, although the outer pads may have areoles with needles on their flat surfaces. Normally, areoles have only one or two large needles surrounded by a few very small ones; they are similar to areoles on *O. phaeacantha*, a taller species.

Where found: Pricklypear is usually found in sandy areas and grassy slopes up into the foothills. This pricklypear species grows abundantly between Albuquerque and Santa Fe.

Pricklypears are used by man and animals for food, drink, and shelter. They are a good source of emergency food and water. Locally, people gather the fruits and make jelly. The pulp of the fruit can be dried and will keep for years. The seeds can also be dried and ground into a meal that is used as a substitute for cornmeal. Young pads, when peeled, may be served either raw or roasted like eggplant. The fruit is sold in Mexico as *tuna* (Spanish for pricklypear).

CLIFF PRICKLYPEAR
Opuntia erinacea

Other names: Utah pricklypear.

Flower: Pink; May to July.

Description: This plant has the flat joints or pads characteristic of pricklypears. Clumps are seldom over 30 cm (12 in) high and 1 m (3 ft) in diameter. The joints are bluish-green, 6 cm (2¼ in) to 9 cm (3½ in) broad, with usually 4 to 6 pad to a stem. Dense spines occur over the entire pad, with upper spines turned downward.

Where found: The cliff pricklypear is found in the grasslands along the Rio Grande and on the mesa west of Albuquerque.

This pricklypear can be used to provide the same benefits as other varieties. Its ethnobotanical importance is minimal, however, because of its small size and scarcity.

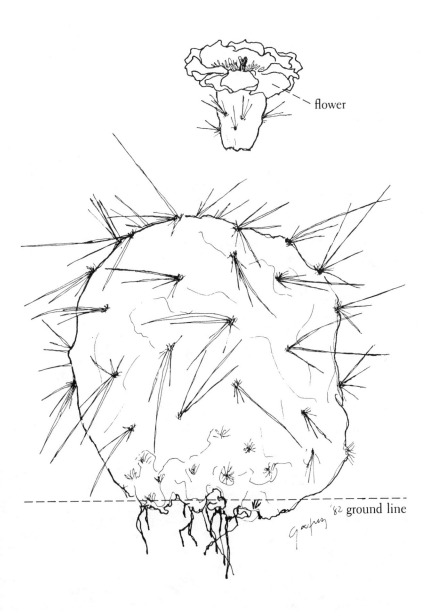

flower

'82 ground line

29

CLARETCUP HEDGEHOG
Echinocereus triglochidiatus

Other names: Hedgehog, crimson hedgehog, mound cactus, heart twister, strawberry cactus.

Flower: Crimson; May to July.

Description: This attractive cactus has one stem but often grows in clumps. There are up to 4 ash-white straight spines in each group of spines (areole). Flowers last several days before wilting. The yellow-green fruit is thin skinned.

Where found: Claretcup hedgehog is found in open grasslands and rocky hillsides up to 2,744 m (9,000 ft) in elevation.

When the claretcup hedgehog is in bloom, it is visible from a considerable distance. The fruit is juicy and edible; it smells like a strawberry. This is a colorful plant for a cactus garden.

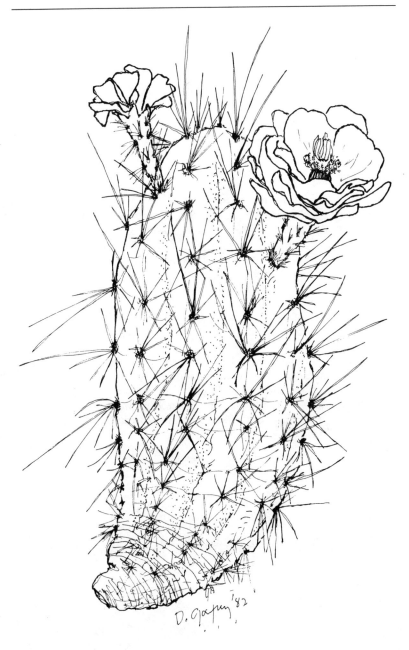

D. Gapuz '82

DATIL YUCCA
Yucca baccata

Other names: Banana yucca, Indian banana, blue yucca, datil.

Flower: Waxy-white; April to July.

Description: This plant has short, thick stems, with leaves densely clustered, 40 cm (16 in) to 75 cm (30 in) long and about 5 cm (2 in) wide. The leaves are rigid, with coarse, stringy fibers along the edges, and very sharp pointed at the tips. A cluster of flowers is 45 cm (18 in) to 1 m (3 ft) long, with flowers 5 cm (2 in) to 15 cm (6 in) in length. The three-celled fruit becomes fleshy and turns yellow or purplish at maturity, much like a short banana. Seeds are many, black, and flat.

Where found: Datil yucca is found often in pinyon and juniper woodlands on the drier slopes, mesas and rocky areas up to 2,439 m (8,000 ft) in elevation.

This plant had many uses among prehistoric peoples. The fibers, stripped from the leaves, were used to make cloth, rope, mats, sandals, and baskets. The young flower stalks, as well as the buds, flowers, and fruits, were used as food. A fermented beverage was made from the fruit and a soap from the roots. Some rural people still find this soap suitable for shampoo.

fruit

SOAPTREE YUCCA
Yucca elata

Other names: Soapweed yucca, palmilla.

Flower: Waxy-white; May to June.

Description: This plant is a narrow, elongated-leafed yucca with a flowering stem that may reach a height of 4.5 to 5 m (15 to 16 ft). The plant usually grows alone, not forming clumps. Leaves are evergreen, spine-tipped with fibers curling from the edges. The stem has numerous blossoms and extends above the leaves. The fruit has three longitudinal sections, each filled with many black, flat seeds.

Where found: This yucca is found in the central and southern parts of New Mexico in dry sandy soils up to approximately 1,829 m (6,000 ft) in elevation.

This is the state flower of New Mexico. There are several species of narrow- or fine-leafed yuccas. Their sizes vary from the low growing Y. *angustissima* to the large Joshua tree, Y. *brevifolia*, of the western deserts. All are eye-catching throughout the year, especially when crowned with the white blossoms. In winter, the evergreen leaves stand out against the drab winter color of other plants. Most yuccas have similar uses such as for food, soap, and as a substitute for jute fibers in making cordage.

SOAPWEED YUCCA
Yucca glauca

Other names: Yucca, small soapweed yucca, narrowleaf yucca.

Flower: White to greenish-white; May and June.

Description: This low yucca has a stem so short that the blossoms may appear to begin at ground level. The leaves are tough, with the usual loose fibers along the edges.

Where found: Soapweed yucca is found on the drier slopes in rocky and sandy sites up to about 2,287 m (7,500 ft) in elevation. It is a common yucca in the Middle Rio Grande Valley.

The soapweed yucca has uses similar to the other narrow-leafed yuccas. All yuccas possess sharp-pointed leaves. They can inflict painful punctures to those who walk carelessly among them.

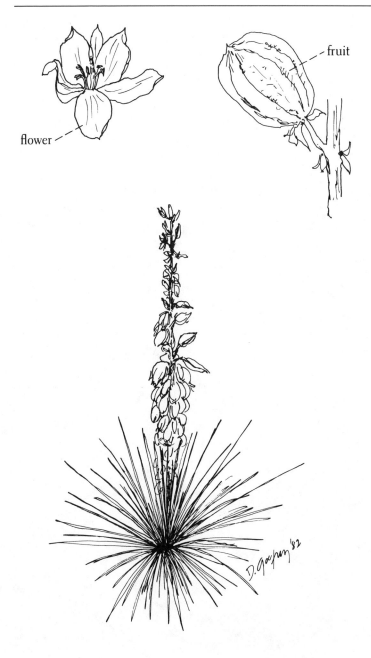

flower

fruit

3

Creepers and Climbers

BUFFALO GOURD
Cucurbita foetidissima

Other names: Coyote melon, calabazilla.

Flower: Yellow, large; May to August.

Description: This gray-green perennial plant has conspicuous trailing stems that reach up to 6 m (20 ft) in length. The tennis-ball-size fruit, 10 cm (4 in) in diameter, are yellowish, striped, and very conspicuous after the leaves have been winter killed. Leaves are triangular, longer than wide, pointed, up to 30 cm (12 in) long, and the upper surface hairy. The blossoms are large, yellow, and trumpet-shaped.

Where found: Buffalo gourd is found throughout the area on the alluvial soils of the mesas up to 2,134 m (7,000 ft) in elevation. In town, it can be seen along arroyos, in empty lots, and along dirt roads.

Southwestern Indians considered buffalo gourd an inferior food but they ate it nevertheless—raw, cooked, dried, or as a mush made from ground seeds. Early settlers crushed the roots and used them as a cleaning agent for clothes. Today, the gourds are used only as ornaments. The buffalo gourd is related to many edible plants such as melons, cucumbers, pumpkins, and squashes.

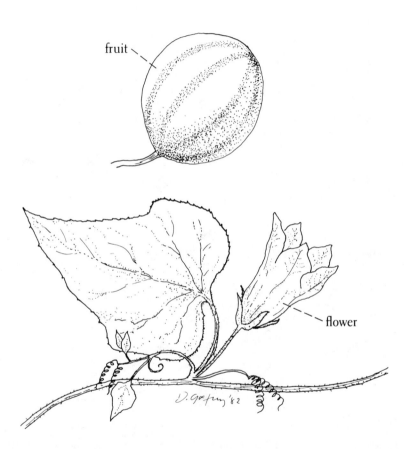

fruit

flower

STRAWBERRY
Fragaria ovalis

Other names: Wild strawberry, wood strawberry.

Flower: White; May to October.

Description: The strawberry is a low, herbaceous plant with hairy, leafless stems, seldom exceeding 20 cm (8 in) in height. The leaves appear at the end of the stalk, and each comprises three coarsely toothed leaflets. The five-petaled flowers are grouped in a small cluster at the end of the leafless stem. Flowers rarely extend beyond the leaves.

Where found: Strawberries thrive in the foothills to the mountains in a variety of soils—dry or moist, loam or clayey—from 2,134 m (7,000 ft) to 3,506 m (11,000 ft) in elevation.

Wild strawberries, a favorite of small animals and birds, are delicious, but it is difficult to find many ripe berries in one spot.

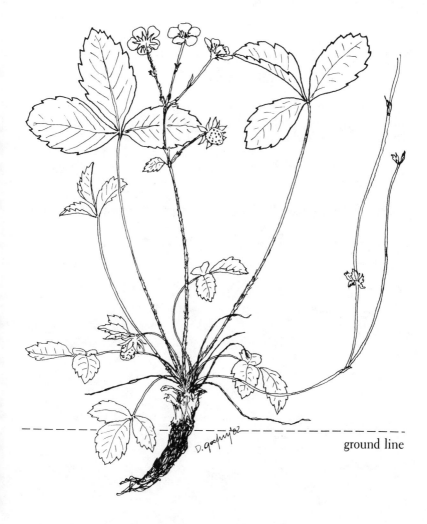

ground line

BINDWEED
Convolvulus arvensis

Other names: Field bindweed.

Flower: White, striped with pink; May to July.

Description: Bindweed is a creeping prostrate plant with dull green arrowhead-shaped leaves. The bottom edges of the leaves spread outward. The flower superficially resembles a small morning glory.

Where found: Bindweed is found in fields, roadsides, empty lots, arroyos, and along sidewalks from the valley to 1,829 m (6,000 ft) in elevation.

This plant can grow thick enough to smother out crop plants. It is hard to eradicate and once started is difficult for farmers to control. An antihemorrhagic has been discovered in bindweed.

PUNCTURE VINE
Tribulus terrestris

Other names: Bullhead, goathead, burnut, caltrop.

Flower: Yellow, small; March to October.

Description: This is an annual plant with long stems radiating out to 1 m (3 ft) from one root. The leaves are pinnately compound (leaflets arranged along a main stalk); each leaf comprises 8 to 12 leaflets. Flowers are small and develop into a flat fruit with two strong spines.

Where found: Puncture vine is found in all areas up to 1,234 m (7,000 ft) in elevation. It grows in lawns, flower gardens, cracks in sidewalks, and along arroyos and street medians.

The stiff, clinging spines of this plant will puncture a bicycle tire but not a car tire. Its Latin name *Tribulus* means "plant with thorns."

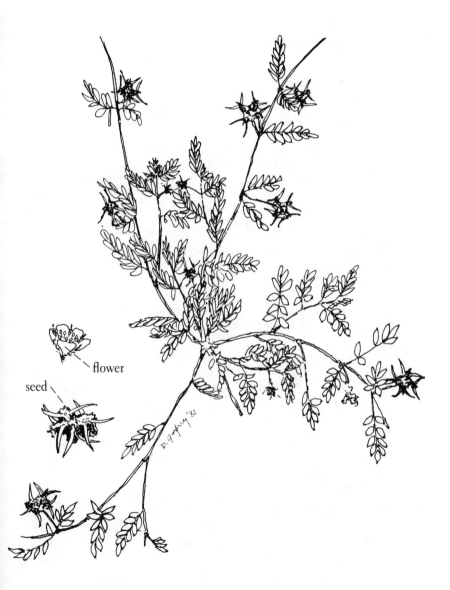

flower

seed

VIRGINIA CREEPER
Parthenocissus inserta

Other names: Woodbine, thicket creeper, American ivy.

Flower: Greenish, small, in open, flat-topped cluster; June and July.

Description: Virginia creeper is a rambling, trailing vine that grows on bushes, trees, and fences. The leading tendrils have no sucking disks. Young stems are red-brown, turning gray with age. The leaves usually consist of 5 leaflets but may have 3 to 7 leaflets; they turn red in the fall. The dark blue berries appear in grape-like bunches, mature in August, and remain on the vine during winter.

Where found: Virginia creeper prefers moist, sunny clearings along fences, roadsides, and stream banks in the Sandias and Manzano mountains, up to 2,134 m (7,000 ft) in elevation.

This plant is sometimes cultivated as an ornamental climbing vine to provide summer shade and colorful fall foliage.

CLEMATIS
Clematis pseudoalpina

Other names: Rocky Mountain clematis, alpine clematis, virgin's bower.

Flower: Lavender; July.

Description: The weak, woody stems of the clematis climb over small trees and bushes with the assistance of tendril-like appendages. The sparsely spaced lavender flowers have four thin sepals. The many seeds have plume-like tails, giving them a feathery appearance. The maple-like leaves are large, consist of three parts, and grow opposite one another along the stem.

Where found: Clematis is usually found in the rich soils of the coniferous forests from 1,829 m (6,000 ft) to 3,049 m (10,000 ft) in elevation.

Several species of *Clematis* are grown as ornamentals. The plume-like tails on the many seeds make this an attractive plant even after the flowers are gone.

seed

D. Gafney '82

4

Trees, Shrubs, and Bushes

LOCUST
Robinia neomexicana

Other names: New Mexico locust, rose locust, pink locust, Southwest locust.

Flower: Purplish-pink; May to July.

Description: Locust can be either a large shrub or a small tree. The thorny limbs may reach a height of 7.5 m (25 ft). Leaves are pinnately compound (several leaflets arranged along the leaf stalk) with one terminal leaflet on the end of the leaf stalk. The compound leaf consists of 9 to 21 oblong leaflets covered with fine hairs. There are two short, stiff spines at the base of the leaf.

Where found: It is found primarily in the mountains in association with ponderosa pine and spruce-fir from 1,220 m (4,000 ft) to 2,744 m (9,000 ft) in elevation. However, it does thrive in the canyons of the foothills or dry rocky sites at the higher elevations as well. Many of these plants grow along New Mexico 44 near the Sandia Peak ski area.

The New Mexico locust is an attractive plant that is effective in retarding soil erosion where it grows.

D. Gaffny '82

CHOKECHERRY
Prunus virginiana

Other names: Western or black chokecherry, capulin.

Flower: White; May and June.

Description: Chokecherry is a large shrub or small tree reaching 7.5 m (25 ft) in height with a trunk 20 cm (8 in) in diameter. The flower has five spreading petals arranged in a showy cluster 5 cm (2 in) to 10 cm (4 in) in length at the end of leafy branchlets. The dark purple, juicy, and slightly tart fruit is about 1 cm ($^3/_8$ in) in diameter. Pointed and finely sawtoothed leaves are arranged alternately on the branches. The top side of the leaves is dark green and smooth; the underside, lighter and hairy.

Where found: Chokecherry is usually found in sunny, moist, or dry sites from the foothills to ponderosa pine forests at 2,591 m (8,500 ft) in elevation.

The genus *Prunus* includes peaches, plums, cherries, apricots, and almonds. Chokecherries are eaten by animals and birds. Chokecherry is an excellent source of fruit for jelly, jam and wine.

flower

fruit

RED ELDERBERRY
Sambucus racemosa

Other names: Red berry elder, scarlet elderberry, bunchberry elder.

Flower: White to yellowish; June and July.

Description: This shrub varies in height from 2 m (6 ft) to 4.5 m (15 ft). Twigs have large white-to-brown pithy centers. Flowers are small and grow in rounded clusters. Leaves usually consist of 7 sharply serrated leaflets. The bright red berries are 6 mm (1/4 in) in diameter and appear in showy clusters.

Where found: Red elderberry is usually found in the moist to wet sites— in valleys, along streams, and in sheltered areas at the bottoms of rocky outcrops from 2,286 m (7,500 ft) to 3,049 m (10,000 ft) in elevation. In the Albuquerque area, it grows in abundance along the road above the Capulin picnic area in the Sandia Mountains.

Elderberries are used for jelly, preserves, and wine. The blue elderberry, *S. glauca*, was a staple food of the Indians and settlers and is still used today. The blue elderberry grows in northern New Mexico. Red elderberries have a tart taste, so it is better to try only a few at first to avoid an upset stomach.

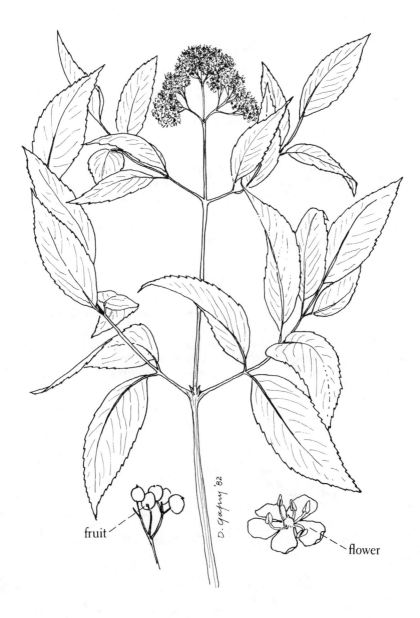

fruit

flower

59

ALGERITA
Berberis Fremontii

Other names: Barberry, hollygrape, palo amarillo, Berbero, Fremont barberry.

Flower: Yellow: May to July.

Description: This many-branched shrub reaches 150 cm (5 ft) to 3 m (10 ft) in height. Three to nine small, yellow flowers grow at the end of the branches. The dark blue berries are small and grape-like, 12 mm (^{1}/$_2$ in) in diameter. Three to seven small leaflets make up each evergreen leaf. The leaflets have a wavy edge with three points on each side. A sharp spine extends from each of the points.

Where found: Algerita is found at elevations up to 2,134 m (7,000 ft) in association with pinyon and juniper trees.

Several species of this plant are used as ornamentals because of their shiny-green, holly-like leaves that turn various shades of red and purple in the winter. The berries make excellent jams and jellies. A brilliant yellow dye for coloring yarn can be obtained from the roots. The Hopi Indians make various articles from the flexible yellow wood of algerita.

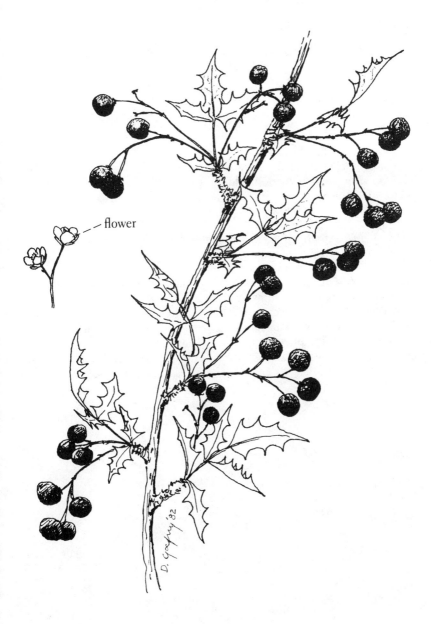

flower

APACHE PLUME
Fallugia paradoxa

Other names: Feather rose, feather duster bush, poñil.

Flower: White with yellow center; April to August.

Description: This shrub grows 1 to 2 m (3 to 6 ft) in height with many slender branches covered with a whitish, shaggy bark. The leaves have three to seven clefts and grow in clusters close to the stem. The five-petaled flower resembles a white wild rose and grows 2.5 cm (1 in) to 4 cm (1½ in) across on slender stalks. Seeds are feathery.

Where found: Apache plume is found along arroyos in the foothills of the Sandia and Manzano mountains.

The name Apache plume is descriptive of the feathery-tailed seeds of the plant, which resemble an Indian warbonnet. The flowers and seed clusters may occur on the bush concurrently. The Hopi Indians use an infusion of the leaves as a stimulant for hair growth. Livestock and wildlife graze on this plant during the winter.

RABBITBRUSH
Chrysothamnus nauseosus

Other names: False goldenrod, chamisa, chamiso blanco, rubber rabbitbrush.

Flower: Yellow; July through September.

Description: This silver-gray shrub is covered with clusters of small yellow flowers in late summer that become white cottony seeds in the fall. The larger stems are woody with a gray-brown bark that sometimes shreds. The smaller branches are covered with matted hairs. Although it may grow taller, the plant normally reaches 60 cm (2 ft) to 150 cm (5 ft) in height.

Where found: It grows up to 2,439 m (8,000 ft) in elevation in the Middle Rio Grande Valley along roadsides, on dry slopes, mesas, and in arroyos.

Rabbitbrush contains rubber latex of fair quality. However, owing to the scarcity of the plant, it is not economically practical to harvest. The flexible stems have been used by the Hopi Indians for making baskets, and the Navajos make a yellow dye from the flowers and a green dye from the inner bark for dying yarn. Rabbitbrush is used extensively in southwestern landscaping.

FOURWING SALTBUSH
Atriplex canescens

Other names: Cenizo, chamizo, chamiza, saltbush, chico, wingscale.

Flower: Pale yellow; summer into fall.

Description: Fourwing saltbush is easily identified most of the year by the distinctive fourwinged pale-brown-to-nearly-white seeds. This woody, gray-green, densely branched shrub grows to 60 cm (24 in) to 1.5 m (5 ft) in height. Leaves are narrow and slightly wider above the middle of the leaf. Flowers grow in clusters near the end of the branches.

Where found: The fourwing saltbush is one of the most common shrubs in the Southwest. It grows in a variety of soils and under many different climatic conditions. It is found in the desert and mountains up to about 2,439 m (8,000 ft) in elevation and appears alongside creosote bush, sagebrush, pinyon, and ponderosa pine.

Fourwing saltbush provides food, shade, and shelter for livestock, wild game, and birds. Man once used the salt-impregnated leaves to flavor other food, and the seeds were ground to make meal. The Hopi Indians are reported to have used the ashes of this plant as a substitute for baking powder. Garden beets, sugar beets, and spinach are members of this family of plants.

seed

CREOSOTE BUSH
Larrea tridentata

Other names: Grease wood, hediondilla (*little stinker* in Spanish).

Flower: Yellow and small; blooms in spring but may flower after a January rain.

Description: Creosote bush is an evergreen shrub with numerous branches that can grow up to 3.5 m (11 ft) tall but usually grow to a height of 1 m (3 ft). The leaves are thick and sticky and smell like creosote. They grow in pairs, united at the base. The bush is covered by small, white, fuzzy seed balls after flowering.

Where found: Creosote bush is found on dry rocky soils up to 1,524 m (5,000 ft) in elevation.

This shrub is used in Southwest landscaping. Creosote bush may cover thousands of acres in a nearly pure stand with most plants a uniform size, but it is not a forage plant. Some Indians have used the lac (resinous crustation) found on the plant to mend pottery.

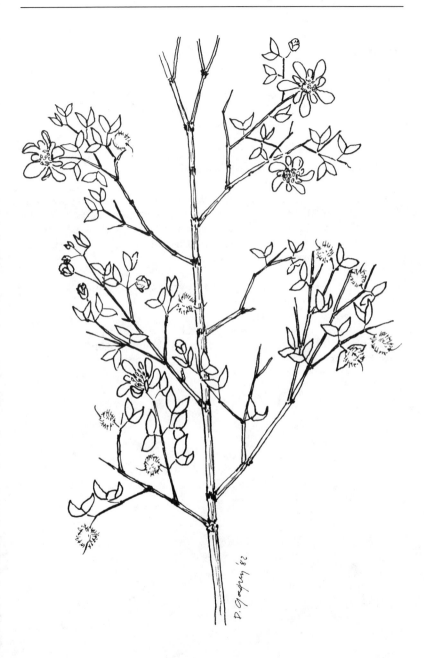

BEEPLANT
Cleome serrulata

Other names: Rocky Mountain beeplant, spider flower, skunkweed, stinking clover.

Flower: Purplish-pink; June to September.

Description: This is a summer plant with branching stems that grow from 30 cm (12 in) to 105 cm (42 in) tall. The leaves have three smooth, bluish-green leaflets that have an unpleasant odor when crushed (hence the name *skunkweed*). The flower heads are purplish-pink to white. The slender, green seed pods hang below the flowers.

Where found: The beeplant is found in grasslands, disturbed areas, arroyos, and on sandy ground up to 2,134 m (7,000 ft) in elevation.

Beeplants will sometimes take over several acres, painting the landscape lavender-purplish-pink. This is a favorite plant of hummingbirds and doves, as well as bees.

FOUR O'CLOCK
Mirabilis multiflora

Other names: Colorado four o'clock.

Flower: Magenta-purple; April to September.

Description: Four o'clocks resemble small shrubs because of their diffuse branching. Leaves are opposite one another on the stem, smooth edged, and dark green with short stalks. Flowers are in groups of three to six in a bell-shaped cluster. The five yellow stamens (pollen bearers) and a purple pistil (ovary bearer) extend beyond the petals.

Where found: This plant is found on mesas, in foothills, along arroyos, and among rock outcroppings up to 2,134 m (7,000 ft) in elevation.

The four o'clock starts blooming in the late afternoon, and by nightfall the plant is covered with a blanket of magenta blossoms. Wild four o'clocks closely resemble the cultivated variety.

SNAKEWEED
Gutierrezia Sarothrae

Other names: Match weed, resin weed, broomweed, turpentine weed, slinkweed, sheepweed.

Flower: Yellow; May to November.

Description: A densely branched, resinous shrub that grows up to 60 cm (2 ft) tall. The main stems are woody and leafless on the lower parts. Leaves are numerous, smooth edged, and bend from the stem. The flowers are small and yellow. They grow in clusters and cover most of the plant.

Where found: Snakeweed is found in dry, stony soils of the arroyos, mesas, and grasslands of this area.

This plant is economically worthless to man and animal. When snakeweed is found growing on good grasslands, overgrazing is indicated. The plant does not slow soil erosion. The names *snakeweed* and *sheepweed* are derived from the practice of applying a poultice of the boiled plant leaves directly to the spot where a sheep was bitten by a rattlesnake. The results are rapidly reduced swelling and a cured animal.

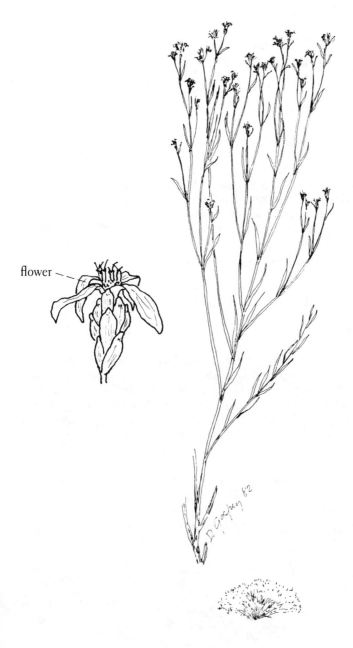

flower

BUSH MORNING GLORY
Ipomoea leptophylla

Other names: Morning glory.

Flower: Magenta; June through September.

Description: This plant is a roundish bush growing from a large taproot (sometimes weighing up to 100 pounds) that may reach 30 cm (1 ft) across and extend 1.3 m (4 ft) into the ground. The stem may be erect, but usually it is somewhat spread out, reaching 30 cm (1 ft) to 1.3 m (4 ft) in length. The leaves are up to 15 cm (6 in) long, and the flowers, like those of the domestic morning glory, are 4 cm (1½ in) to 7.5 cm (3 in) long, varying from magenta to rose shades of pink.

Where found: This small bush may be found in sandy soils from 1,372 m (4,500 ft) to 2,134 m (7,000 ft) in elevation. In the Albuquerque area, bush morning glory may be seen along New Mexico 44 between San Felipe and Zia pueblos.

Not only is the taproot of this plant a good survival food, it may be used any time. Tender, crisp, and sweet, it makes an excellent salad ingredient or may be munched raw like a carrot. It may also be boiled or baked like a potato. When sun-dried, the root will maintain its flavor and texture for several months. Bush morning glory is ideally adapted to the arid Southwest, for it can withstand prolonged drought because of its large taproot.

WILD ROSE
Rosa Woodsii

Other names: Wood's rose, Fendler's rose.

Flower: Pink; July and August.

Description: The wild rose is a shrub with thorny, reddish stems and pink flowers. The flowers grow to 5 cm (2 in) across and are showy, fragrant, and mostly solitary. The red fruit resembles a miniature apple.

Where found: It is found throughout the region in partially shaded areas along streams and in pine forests from 1,220 m (4,000 ft) to 2,744 m (9,000 ft) in elevation.

Roses provide food and shelter for man and wildlife. The rose "hip," or fruit, is high in vitamins A and C, particularly vitamin C. Wildlife graze the plants, and birds eat the fruits. The dense thicket provides shelter to small mammals and birds.

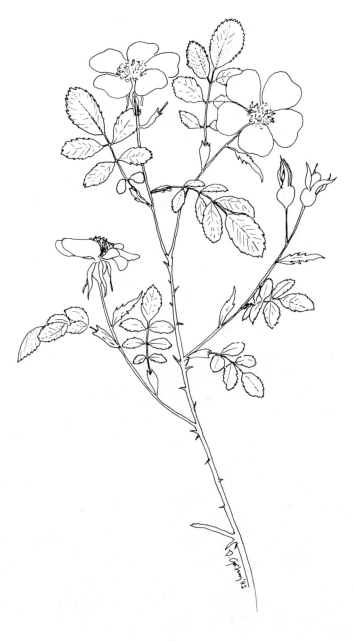

5

Flowering Plants by Color

CURLY DOCK
Rumex hymenosepalus

Other names: Dock, curled dock, sour dock, wild rhubarb, canaigre.

Flower: Inconspicuous; April to June. (Fruit is conspicuous and reddish.)

Description: One of the first plants to grow green in the spring, dock stands out among the brown and tan winter coloring of the other dormant plants. Dock is a perennial plant with a large taproot and stems from 30 cm (1 ft) to 1 m (3 ft) tall, capped with reddish, three-winged seeds. The wide leaves are long, with wavy, wilted-looking edges.

Where found: Curly dock is found throughout Albuquerque and the Rio Grande Valley along arroyos and roads and in empty lots.

This is a good survival plant to know, as the entire plant may be eaten when young. Young tender leaves, gathered in the spring and prepared like spinach, are considered by many midwesterners and southerners excellent as a pot herb or salad greens. Dock is also known as wild rhubarb, and the stems can be used as a substitute for rhubarb.

EVENING PRIMROSE
Oenothera caespitosa

Other names: Stemless primrose, sandlily, tufted evening primrose.

Flower: White; April to August.

Description: Evening primrose is a seemingly stemless white flowered plant. The four large, white petals with a tinge of pink make this an attractive blossom.

Where found: This plant is widespread throughout the area but especially conspicuous along roads in sandy soils up to 2,286 m (7,500 ft) in elevation as well as in empty lots and along sidewalks within the city.

The flowers can be seen early in the morning. They open in the late evening or at night, last only a few hours after sunrise, and turn pinkish as they wilt. The leaves and roots of this plant can be used in salads but may be slightly tart for some tastes.

YERBA MANSA
Anemopsis californica

Other names: Lizard's tail.

Flower: White; May to August.

Description: A herbaceous, perennial plant with large, fleshy leaves that are mostly basal, heart-shaped at the stem. The solitary flower grows on a short stalk that is seldom over 15 cm (6 in) in height.

Where found: Yerba mansa is found along the Rio Grande in wet, swampy, or saline areas, often in standing water.

This plant grows profusely and covers large areas. It is reported that Pima Indians and early day Californians of Spanish descent used an infusion made from the roots for various ailments.

ground line

YARROW
Achillea lanulosa

Other names: Western yarrow, milfoil, wild tansy, woolly yarrow.

Flower: White, in flat-topped clusters; June to September.

Description: The unbranched, erect stems of this plant grow up to 1 m (3 ft) in height and are covered by dense, white-woolly hairs. Long, narrow leaves are divided and subdivided into fern-like foliage. The upper leaves grow directly out of the stem. Small flower heads are numerous in compact, branched, mostly flat-topped clusters.

Where found: Yarrow is found among sagebrush, in canyon bottoms, arroyos, aspen groves, roadsides, and vacant lots up to 3,500 m (11,500 ft) in elevation.

The generic name *Achillea* refers to the Greek hero Achilles, who is credited with first using yarrow to cure wounds. *Lanulosa*, the Latin word for *woolly*, describes the fine, silky hairs covering the plant stems. Some Indian tribes have considered yarrow a potent love charm.

SOLOMON PLUME
Smilacina stellata

Other names: Starry solomon plume, starflower, false solomon's seal.

Flower: White; May and June.

Description: The unbranched, leafy stems grow from thick, spreading rootstocks. The long, narrow leaves droop slightly at the top, are smooth edged, and have multiple veins. The flowers have 6 petals each and grow in open clusters. Berries are green with dark blue stripes. The plant normally grows 60 cm (24 in) tall but may reach a meter (3 ft) in height.

Where found: Solomon plume is usually found in the rich soils of the cool, shaded sites of coniferous forests from 1,829 m (6,000 ft) to 3,049 m (10,000 ft) in elevation. It grows in abundance in the Sandia and Manzano mountains.

The tender young shoots may be prepared like asparagus. The bittersweet-tasting berries are edible, raw or cooked. They should be eaten in small amounts at first as they may act as a laxative when eaten in quantity.

ground line

CLAMMYWEED
Polanisia trachysperma

Other names: Roughseed clammyweed.

Flower: White to pale-yellow; June to September.

Description: Clammyweed is an annual, unpleasant-smelling plant with erect, branched stems that are clammy or sticky to the touch. The leaves are trifoliate with three oblong or narrow leaflets. The purple stamens are numerous and extend beyond the white-to-pale-yellow petals, giving the flower a pinkish-lavender appearance. The fruit is elongated, flat, and short stalked.

Where found: Clammyweed is usually found in the sand or gravel bottoms of arroyos and dry streambeds up to 1,982 m (6,500 ft) in elevation.

This plant resembles yellow spider flower (*Cleome lutea*) and jackass clover (*Wislizenia refracta*). However, the seeds of clammyweed grow upward, while the others hang down.

PRICKLY POPPY
Argemone hispida

Other names: Thistle poppy, chicalote, fried egg plant.

Flower: White with yellow-orange center; spring to fall.

Description: The large prickly poppy flowers have four to six petals and can grow from 5 cm (2 in) to 12 cm (5 in) across. The blossom contains many yellow-orange stamens. Stems and leaves are covered with short, fine needles. The yellow sap from the plant is acrid.

Where found: Prickly poppy, a drought-resistant plant, is found in dry soils up to 2,439 m (8,000 ft) in elevation. In the city, it thrives in empty lots and on the banks of arroyos.

This plant is ignored by animals because of its unpleasant sap and the dense spine cover. As a result, it has taken over some areas. The acrid yellow sap is reported to have been used by Indians and early settlers to treat some skin diseases. The seeds are a favorite food of doves.

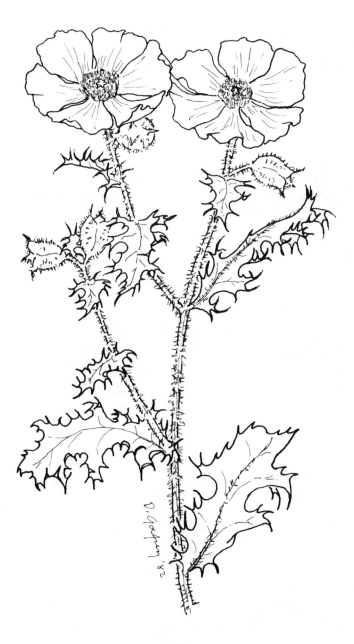

BEARGRASS
Nolina microcarpa

Other names: Basketgrass, nolina.

Flower: Creamy-tan; May and June.

Description: Beargrass is a large clump of grass with flowering stems. The leaves, often dried at the ends, may exceed 60 cm (2 ft) in length. Stems may reach a height of 2.5 m (8 ft). The plume-like flowering section of the stem can grow to more than 30 cm (1 ft) in length.

Where found: This plant is found in rocky, exposed locations in the foothills up to 1,982 m (6,500 ft) in elevation.

Bears occasionally dig up and eat the tuberous roots of this plant, hence the name *beargrass*. The plant has many uses. Mexicans use the leaves for weaving basket handles. Stems, roots, and the emerging flower stalks can be prepared for food in the same way as the stems, roots, and flowering stalks of the yucca. Livestock and wildlife will graze on beargrass only in times of drought. Beargrass is used occasionally in southwestern landscaping.

flower

stem

LOUSEWORT
Pedicularis Parryi

Other names: Parry lousewort, Parry pedicularis, fern leaf, wood betony.

Flower: Whitish with pink lines; June to September.

Description: A single stemmed plant that reaches to 50 cm (20 in) in height. Most of the fern-like leaves grow from the base of the plant, but a few appear along the flowering stem. The upper lip of the flower is curved and hood-shaped.

Where found: Lousewort is usually found in the shaded soils of the coniferous forests from 2,286 m (7,500 ft) to 3,658 m (12,000 ft) in elevation. The aspen groves and cool northern exposures of the Sandia and Manzano mountains are a likely place to find this plant.

The generic name is derivative of the Latin word *pediculus* meaning louse. The seeds of lousewort were used in Roman times to kill lice.

CRANESBILL GERANIUM
Geranium Richardsonii

Other names: Richardson geranium.

Flower: White with a slight purple tinge; April to October.

Description: A tall slender plant that grows up to 75 cc (30 in) tall with leaves that are palmately parted (like fingers) into five deeply cleft segments. The flowers have five petals. The bottom half of each petal is covered with short hair. Purple-tipped hairs also appear on the flower stalk.

Where found: Cranesbill geranium is usually found in open areas from 1,982 m (6,500 ft) to 3,506 m (11,500 ft) in elevation. It is seldom found in the shady coniferous forest.

The term *Geranium* is from the Greek word *geranos* (crane) and is descriptive of the long beak on the seed. The roots and rhizomes have been used medicinally as astringents.

D. Gaspry '82

ALUMROOT
Heuchera pulchella

Other names: Coral bell.

Flower: Pink; June to October.

Description: A small, perennial plant whose scaly lower stem is woody at the base. Leaves grow mostly from the base of the plant and are indented at the base. They have a long stalk and toothed edges. Flowers, when in bloom, appear to grow from only one side of the stem. The petals are longer than the bracts.

Where found: Alumroot is usually found in moist, shady, rocky sites in coniferous forests from 1,982 m (6,500 ft) to 3,658 m (12,000 ft) in elevation. In the Sandias, this plant grows among the rocks by the steps leading from the upper tramway terminal to the restaurant.

The roots of this plant have astringent properties and were used by Indians and settlers to treat diarrhoea caused by drinking alkaline water.

ground line

FAIRYSLIPPER ORCHID
Calypso bulbosa

Other names: Calypso orchid.

Flower: Pink to light purple; June and July.

Description: A low single-stemmed plant that grows from 10 cm (4 in) to 20 cm (8 in) in height. Each stem has one leaf at the base and one blossom. The leaf is broad and oval. The flower has a boat-shaped lower lip striped with a darker color. The lower lip sometimes has yellow hairs.

Where found: The fairyslipper orchid is usually found in cool, moist sites in the spruce or fir forests or aspen groves from 2,439 m (8,000 ft) to 3,200 m (10,500 ft) in elevation. In the Albuquerque area it can be found along the Sandia Crest Trail between the Crest and the upper tramway terminal.

This beautiful, delicate, small plant is one of ten genera of orchids found in the Southwest. Several, including the fairyslipper, flourish in the Sandia Mountains in the Nine-mile picnic area. All orchids are on the endangered species list and should not be picked. They are delicate and will wilt within minutes after picking. They are intolerant of any change in their habitat and will not survive transplanting.

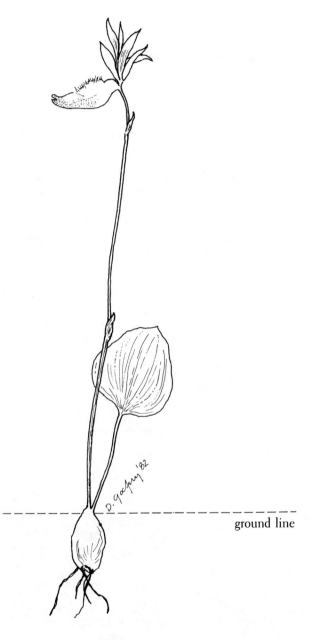

ground line

BEARDTONGUE PENSTEMON
Penstemon Palmeri

Other names: Palmer penstemon, wild snapdragon, pink penstemon.

Flower: Pinkish with darker pink stripes; spring to September.

Description: A short plant, usually not exceeding 60 cm (24 in) in height, with two-lipped pinkish flowers. The leaves are opposite one another along the stem. The flower has one elongated stamen covered with yellowish hairs, hence the name *beardtongue.*

Where found: The beardtongue penstemon is usually found in sandy arroyos and along roads in sagebrush and pinyon areas of the foothills up to 1,982 m (6,500 ft) in elevation.

Beardtongue penstemon is a fragrant addition to any wildflower garden.

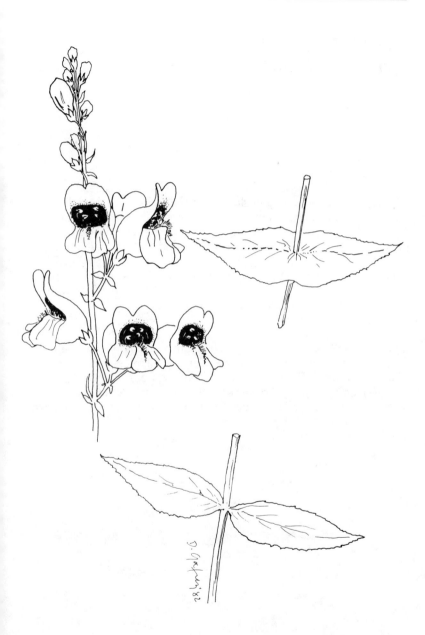

GLOBE MALLOW
Sphaeralcea incana

Other names: Sore eye poppy, wild hollyhock.

Flower: Dark pink to apricot; spring to late autumn.

Description: Globe mallow has a wand-like stem varying in height up to 1.5 m (5 ft) tall. The stem and leaves are covered with soft, short hairs. Flowers usually appear in a single, unbranched, elongated flowering head. Accurate identification is difficult for the occasional botanist because the habitat of this plant overlaps with that of the juniper globe mallow (*S. digitata*) and because of color variations within each species.

Where found: This plant is found in the open grasslands, on sandy or gravelly mesas, or on slopes from 1,220 m (4,000 ft) to 1,829 m (6,000 ft) in elevation. In the city, globe mallow is seen in empty lots, along arroyos, and in street medians.

Globe mallows are common and abundant throughout the Southwest. Colors may be white, pale yellow, lavender, apricot, pink, or red depending upon the species. The name *sore eye poppy* is from the Mexican name *male de ojos.* In contrast, Arizona's Pima Indian name for this plant means "a cure for sore eyes." The mallow family includes hibiscus, cotton, okra, and the domestic hollyhock.

FIREWEED
Epilobium angustifolium

Other names: Willowweed, blooming sally.

Flower: Rose to lilac; July to September.

Description: Fireweed averages 1 m (3 ft) in height but may grow 2 m (6 ft) tall. The flowers have four distinctly separate petals and grow in a pointed cluster. The flower buds droop, but flowers and seed pods are erect. Long, narrow, lance-shaped leaves are 20 cm (8 in) long. They grow without a stalk, directly from the stem. The top side of the leaf is dark green; the bottom side is light green.

Where found: Fireweed is found in burned areas as well as in forest openings, cultivated fields, roadsides, and along streams and dry arroyos.

When mature the long seed pods open and the plant appears to be topped with a cotton tuft. Numerous seeds are then released that are carried great distances by wind. Fireweed is commonly found in the Nine Mile picnic area in the Sandia Mountains.

SWEET WILLIAM
Verbena Wrightii

Other names: Vervain, verbena, Dakota verbena.

Flower: Lavender; May to September

Description: The flowers have no stalks. They grow in elongated spikes, usually in compound or head-like clusters. The individual blossoms appear to be flat, with five petals. Each petal is indented at the tip. The *Verbena* species are difficult to distinguish as hybridization occurs frequently within this genus.

Where found: Sweet william is usually found in open pinyon-juniper woodlands and foothills up to 3,049 m (10,000 ft) in elevation.

The rich lavender color of the flowers makes this a beautiful and showy plant especially when growing in large clumps or among other spring and summer flowers. Common along roadsides, sweet william is also popular in wildflower gardens.

THISTLE
Cirsium neomexicanum

Other names: New Mexico thistle, bull thistle.

Flower: Lavender; March to September.

Description: The woolly stems of the thistle vary from 30 cm (12 in) to nearly 2 m (6 ft) in height. The prickly leaves grow alternately on the stems and are usually toothed. The flowerhead resembles an inverted bundle of straws.

Where found: Thistle is found throughout the Southwest up to 1,982 m (6,500 ft) in elevation.

Indians and early explorers used the thistle as emergency food. The young leaves may be eaten raw as a salad or cooked as potherbs. The young stems should be peeled before eating; they are good either raw or cooked. Thistle-leaf tea can be purchased from stores that carry specialty foods.

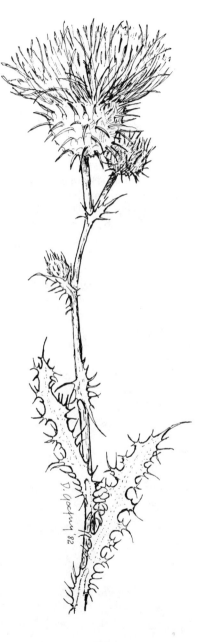

TANSY ASTER
Aster Bigelovii

Other names: Bigelow aster, Christmas daisy, New Mexico aster.

Flower: Lavender-violet; March to November.

Description: This aster may vary from 20 cm (8 in) to 1 m (3 ft) in height. The smooth-edged to deep-cleft leaves grow on alternate sides of the stem. Asters are often confused with fleabane daisies, although there are several ways to distinguish between the two. Asters have several rows of bracts below the flower petals while fleabanes have only one or two rows. The petals of the asters are broader and sparser than those of the fleabane.

Where found: The tansy aster is found throughout the area up to 2,134 m (7,000 ft) in elevation. It is often seen in empty lots, street medians, along sidewalks, or any other waste or disturbed area.

In the fall, the blooming aster, rabbitbrush, and snakeweed color empty lots, mesas, and sidewalks lavender, gold, and yellow. Livestock and wildlife graze on aster, and birds like the seeds.

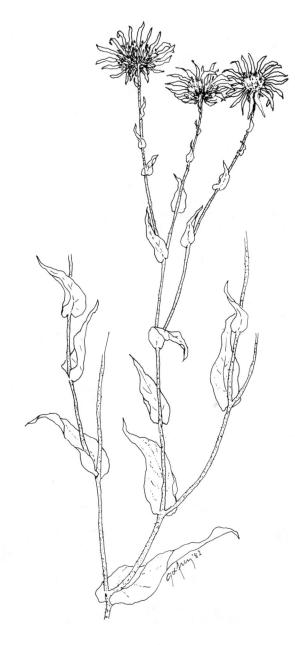

JACOB'S LADDER
Polemonium delicatum

Other names: Skunkleaf polemonium, blue skunkleaf.

Flower: Violet-blue; June to August.

Description: The numerous slender, hairy stems of Jacob's ladder grow out laterally from the base of the plant and then become erect, reaching 30 cm (12 in) in height and growing in bunches. The 5 tubular flower petals are whitish below the middle and violet-blue above the middle. Leaves grow opposite one another on the stem in a ladder-like arrangement.

Where found: Jacob's ladder is found from 2,744 m (9,000 ft) to 3,658 m (12,000 ft) in elevation. In the Albuquerque area it grows near the top or crest of the Sandia Mountains.

The leaves have a strong odor, hence the name *skunkleaf*. This plant is easily started from scattered seeds and is attractive in wildflower gardens.

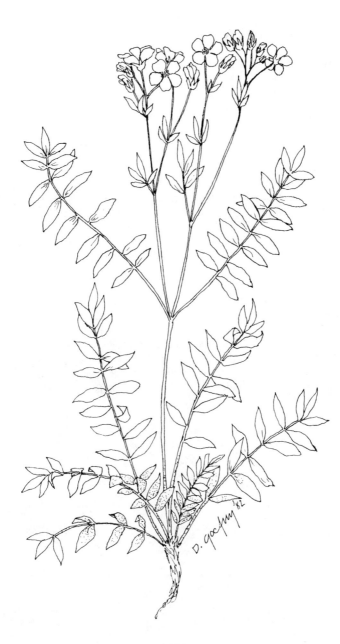

SPIKE VERBENA
Verbena Macdougalii

Other names: None.

Flower: Bluish-violet; June to September.

Description: Superficially spike verbena does not look like a verbena. The violet blossoms occur along several vertical spikes clustered atop a square stem that varies from 30 cm (12 in) to 40 cm (16 in) in height. This plant grows in large clumps.

Where found: Spike verbena is usually found in pinyon foothills and pine forests up to 2,287 m (7,500 ft) in elevation as well as along roads and other disturbed areas.

The square stems with leaves growing opposite one another and the two-lipped flowers may mislead the amateur botanist into thinking this plant is a mint. Remember, "all mints have square stems, but all square stems are not mints." Mints have a characteristic odor when crushed, and the flowers grow in clusters at the top of the stem or in groups along the stem at the base of the leaves. Mint leaves are usually long and narrow. Verbena leaves are irregular in shape.

leaf

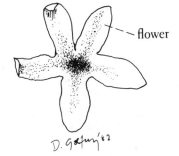

flower

D. Gafney '82

LUPINE
Lupinus argenteus

Other names: Bluebonnet, wolfbane, quakerbonnet, silvery lupine.

Flower: Bluish to purple; June to October.

Description: The pea-like blossoms appear in spikes at the end of leafy stems. The leaves appear to radiate from a common point. The flower is two-lipped with the upper petals curved. The seed pods are compressed and are constricted between seeds.

Where found: Lupine is found along roads and open forests up to 3,049 m (10,000 ft) in elevation.

There are many species of lupine, and it is difficult to distinguish between them. One species, the bluebonnet, is the state flower of Texas. Seeds of a few species contain alkaloids that are poisonous to livestock, especially sheep. The lupine is an attractive and beneficial plant. Like other members of the pea family, it takes nitrogen from the air and releases it into the soil.

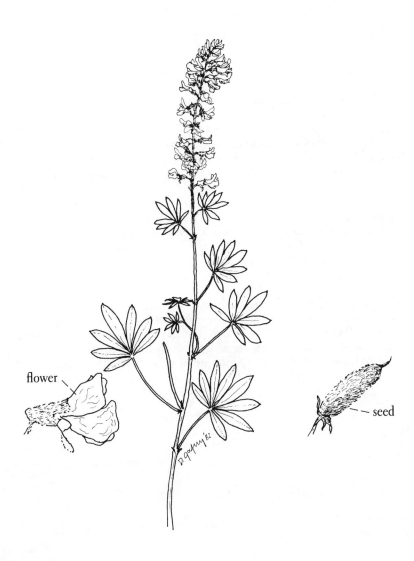

flower

seed

CHICORY
Cichorium intybus

Other names: Succory

Flower: Blue; late spring and summer.

Description: Chicory is a tall, branched plant, 30 cm (1 ft) to 1 m (3 ft) in height, topped by numerous bright flowers 2.5 cm (1 in) to 4 cm (1¼ in) across. The basal leaves, 5 cm (2 in) to 15 cm (5 in) long, spread on the ground and are spatulate in outline. Leaves along the stem are smaller, lanceolate or oblong in shape, with either lobed or smooth edges.

Where found: This plant is found mainly along roads in moist areas or places with relatively heavy rainfall. The flower opens at dawn and closes by mid morning. An early morning drive into the Jemez Mountains between Jemez Pueblo and Jemez Springs will provide an opportunity to see this attractive blue-flowered plant.

Chicory is well known as a substitute for coffee. It can also be added to coffee. To use as a beverage, dig up the roots at any season and, after peeling off the outer layer, slice, roast in the oven until brown, then grind into a powder, which you can brew alone or with your coffee. Young roots may be boiled and eaten like carrots or parsnips. The popular salad plant curly endive belongs to this genus.

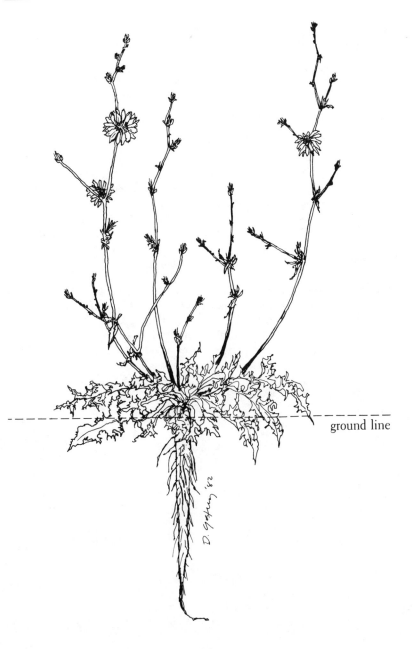

ground line

DALEA
Dalea scoparia

Other names: Indigo bush, peabush.

Flower: Blue, indigo; March to June.

Description: This is a light gray-green plant with branched, rigid stems. Small, bluish flowers appear at the end of the branches. From a distance, the plant may appear to be leafless.

Where found: Dalea is found throughout the area in arroyos and along roads up to 1,829 m (6,000 ft) in elevation. It is common along New Mexico 44 west of Bernalillo.

Dalea has several uses. A yellow dye used for baskets was obtained from the twigs of *D. Emoryi* by the Indians of southwestern Arizona. The Hopi ate the root of *D. terminalis* as a sweet. This species, *D. scoparia*, has been suggested for use in control of soil erosion.

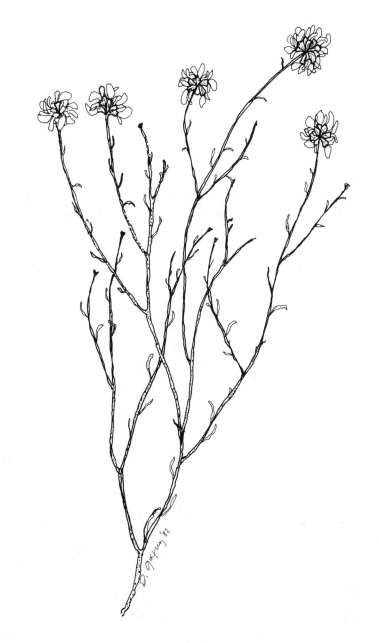

GAILLARDIA
Gaillardia pulchella

Other names: Blanket flower, firewheel.

Flower: Petals are yellow at tips and purple at base; center is purple; April to September.

Description: This plant reaches about 30 cm (12 in) in height, and flower color (see above) is the best way to identify it. The petals are toothed, and the leaves are alternate (not opposite one another on the stem) and hairy. Lower leaves are lobed, and the upper ones narrow and taper to the tip.

Where found: Gaillardia is normally found in pinyon and juniper woodlands and grasslands from 1,067 m (3,500 ft) to 1,677 m (5,500 ft) in elevation.

The cultivated gaillardias are derived from this species of attractive and colorful wild gaillardia.

WHIPPLE BEARDTONGUE
Penstemon Whippleanus

Other names: Dusky beardtongue, purple penstemon.

Flower: Dark purple or wine colored; July and August.

Description: This plant seldom exceeds 60 cm (24 in) in height. However, at higher elevations, it may grow to less than 30 cm (12 in). The lower lip of the blossom projects beyond the upper lip. Leaves grow opposite one another and may be minutely toothed.

Where found: In the Albuquerque area it is found along Sandia Crest. Its range is the mountains and dry areas from 1,982 m (6,500 ft) to 3,658 m (12,000 ft) in elevation.

Whipple beardtongue, one of the larger flowered penstemons, grows in clumps and is ideal for cultivation. A whitish or pale yellow phase occurs occasionally.

TANSY MUSTARD
Descurainia pinnata

Other names: Flixweed.

Flower: Yellow or whitish, small; early spring into summer.

Description: Tansy mustard stems grow often up to 75 cm (30 in) tall with few branches. The leaves are deeply cleft and fern-like. Flowers are small with four petals. The seed pods may vary in length up to 2.5 cm (1 in) long, but they are always round and narrow.

Where found: Tansy mustard is found in disturbed areas in grasslands, valleys, and foothills up to 2,134 m (7,000 ft) in elevation.

Tansy mustard could be used as an emergency food even though it has a strong taste. Some southwestern Indians use the young tender growth as a potherb and make a mush from the parched and ground seeds. In Mexico, the seeds are used in preparing poultices for wounds.

flower

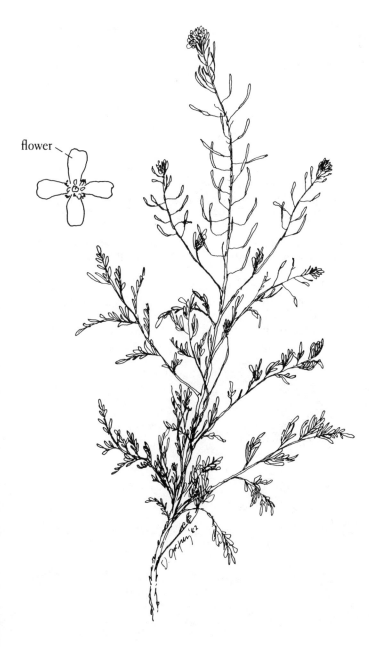

STICKLEAF MENTZELIA
Mentzelia pumila

Other names: Stickleaf, evening star, moonflower, blazingstar.

Flower: Yellow or yellow-cream; May to August.

Description: This many-branched plant reaches 30 cm (1 ft) to 90 cm (3 ft) in height. Stems are whitish and shiny. The leaves are linear, with deep, wavy margins. Stiff hairs (nonstinging) cover the leaves and stems. The flower has ten petals.

Where found: Stickleaf mentzelia is found along roads, arroyos, or where other vegetation has been disturbed up to 2,134 m (7,000 ft) in elevation.

The star-shaped flowers, inconspicuous most of the day, open in the late afternoon. The minute barbed hairs on the leaves and stems stick to clothing, hence the name *stickleaf*. This plant is suitable for wildflower gardens because of its long blooming period as well as its attractive flowers.

D. Gafny '82

CUTLEAF CONEFLOWER
Rudbeckia laciniata

Other names: Split leaf coneflower, coneflower.

Flower: Yellow with greenish-yellow center; July to September.

Description: A tall, branched plant crowned with flowers having yellow petals that appear to lay backwards. The leaves grow alternately on the stem. The lower leaves have three to five deeply separated lobes and the upper leaves are divided into three parts.

Where found: The cutleaf coneflower is usually found along streams in ponderosa pine forests up to 2,591 m (8,500 ft) in elevation. However, it thrives in the rich soil of the coniferous forest along the highway to the Sandia Peak Ski Area.

This showy plant is sometimes mistaken for a sunflower.

D. Gafny '82

DANDELION
Taraxacum officinale

Other names: None.

Flower: Yellow; April to September.

Description: This bright yellow flowered plant is a perennial whose tap-roots may go as deep as 18 inches into the soil. The fleshy parts exude a milky juice when cut or broken. The flower stems are short, 5 cm (2 in) to 30 cm (12 in) long. The leaves are clustered at ground level. The flowers are yellow, one to a stalk, and are 1 cm (¹/₂ in) to 5 cm (2 in) wide. When mature, the yellow flower becomes gray. At this time the seeds are easily distributed by the wind as each has a miniature parachute of hairs.

Where found: Dandelion is found everywhere—especially in lawns. However, it is also abundant in meadows, even above 3,048 m (10,000 ft).

The name *dandelion* is derived from the French "dent de lion"—lion's tooth. Fold the leaves; if you use your imagination, they may resemble a lion's teeth. Usually considered a weed when found in the lawn, the dandelion is actually an attractive and useful plant. The blossom resembles a small chrysanthemum. Young dandelions are delicious when cooked as spinach or can add a tartness to a salad. Dandelion wine is popular with home wine-makers.

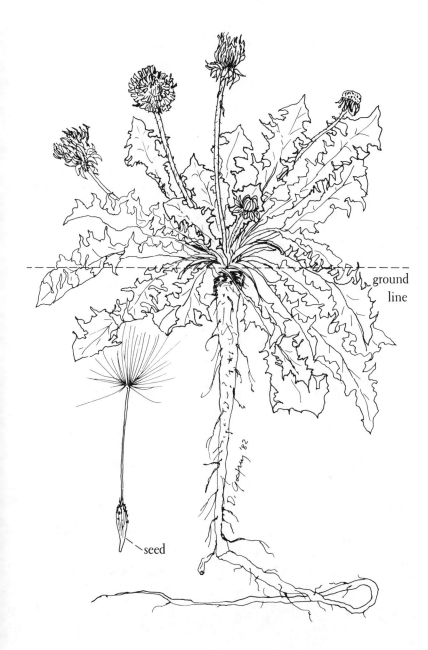

ground
line

seed

139

YELLOW SWEETCLOVER
Melilotus officinalis

Other names: Honey clover, yellow melilot, sweetclover.

Flower: Yellow; July to October.

Description: These leafy plants have branched stems and can grow to 150 cm (5 ft) in height. Leaves are trifoliate with three, toothed leaflets. Seed pods are 6 mm (¹/4 in) long. The herbage is fragrant when dried.

Where found: Yellow sweetclover is found along roads where it has been planted to retard soil erosion.

This tall, fragrant plant, introduced into this country from Europe, is eaten by livestock and wildlife. It makes an excellent honey plant.

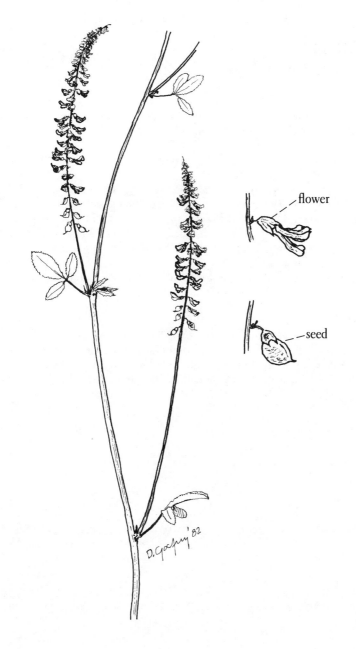

flower

seed

MULLEIN
Verbascum Thapsus

Other names: Flannel mullein, flannel leaf mullein, common mullein, woolly mullein, torchweed, candelaria.

Flower: Yellow; throughout the summer.

Description: The singular tall, coarse, leafy stems usually grow in colonies. The yellow flowers consist of five unequal lobes and grow in elongated spikes. The entire flowering spike is rarely in bloom at one time. Leaves are without stalks; their bases grow directly from the stem. A thick covering of woolly hairs gives the leaves a felt-like appearance and touch.

Where found: Mullein is found along roadsides and in arroyos up to 2,439 m (8,000 ft) in elevation.

Mullein was introduced into this country from Sicily. Early Spanish explorers used dried mullein leaves as a tobacco substitute. It is reported that the inhaled smoke of burning mullein leaves relieves asthma. Ancient Romans dipped the mullein stalks in tallow to make lampwicks or torches; this may be why the Spaniards call it *candelaria* and the English *torchweed*.

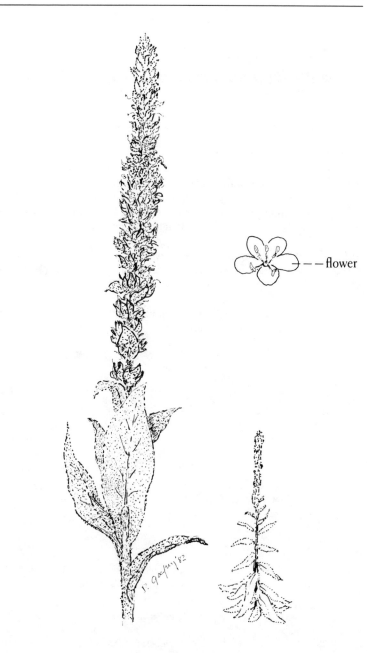

flower

ALPINE SUNFLOWER
Helianthella quinquenervis

Other names: Aspen sunflower, five-nerved helianthella.

Flower: Yellow; July to October.

Description: This usually solitary sunflower grows to 7.5 cm (3 in) to 15 cm (6 in) across on stems that may reach 1.5 m (5 ft) in height. The narrow, five-veined leaves grow opposite along the stem. The leaves reach 10 cm (4 in) to 25 cm (10 in) in length and taper to the tip.

Where found: The alpine sunflower is usually found in mountain meadows and open woods from 1,524 m (5,000 ft) to 3,049 m (10,000 ft) in elevation.

Livestock and wildlife graze on the flowering heads of the *Helianthella*. This plant reproduces only from seed.

GOLDENROD
Solidago sparsiflora

Other names: Yellow weed.

Flower: Yellow, clustered in a curving, plume-like spike; June to October.

Description: This species of goldenrod varies from 30 cm (12 in) to 60 cm (24 in) in height. Its three-ribbed, bluish-green leaves are dull and narrow. The leaves are usually smooth edged, but may be toothed occasionally. Leaves at the base of the stem are larger than those growing in the middle and upper portions of the stem.

Where found: Goldenrod is found along roads and arroyos and in juniper woodlands, mountain meadows, and pine forests up to 2,591 m (8,500 ft) in elevation.

This is the most attractive of the goldenrods found in this area. The sap of goldenrods contains a small amount of rubber.

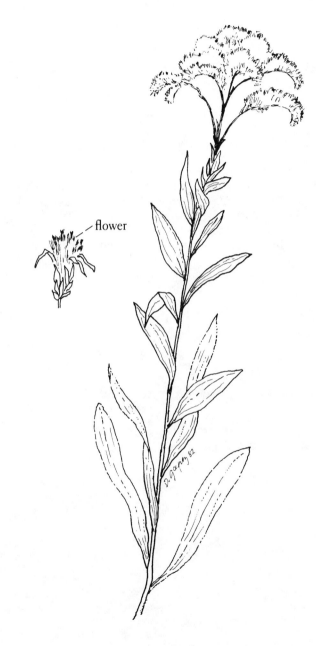

flower

WILD ZINNIA
Zinnia grandiflora

Other names: Plains zinnia, Rocky Mountain zinnia.

Flower: Bright yellow; June to October.

Description: The wild zinnia is a low-growing, woody-based perennial with single flowers blooming at the ends of short branches. Petals are broad and about 19 mm (³/₄ in) long. The narrow, semi-rigid, three-ribbed leaves grow opposite one another along the stem.

Where found: This plant is found with pinyon and juniper trees on dry slopes, mesas, and roadsides from 1,220 m (4,000 ft) to 1,982 m (6,500 ft) in elevation. Coneflowers and verbenas are also found where wild zinnias grow.

This hardy flower is an attractive addition in the flower garden. The popular garden zinnia (Z. *elegans*) is native to Mexico.

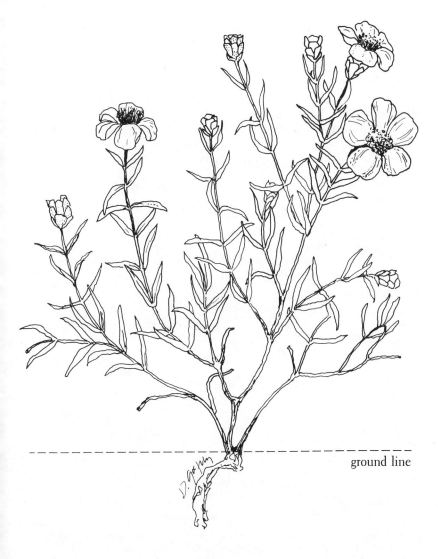

ground line

GOATSBEARD
Tragopogon dubius

Other names: Salsify, goat dandelion.

Flower: Yellow to yellow-orange; June and July.

Description: Goatsbeard is a medium-sized plant that grows from 30 cm (1 ft) to 1 meter (3 ft) tall and resembles a large dandelion. The leaves are long and grasslike, smooth edged, and clasp the stem at the base of the leaf. The flower heads are large and solitary on hollow stalks. The 8 to 13 elongated bracts extend beyond the flower.

Where found: Goatsbeard is found on waste or disturbed areas from 1,067 m (3,500 ft) to 2,134 m (7,000 ft) in elevation. It also grows in flower gardens and along the edges of lawns.

This plant closely resembles a dandelion in all stages of growth. Each seed is attached to a feathery parachute and, like dandelion seeds, may be carried a considerable distance by the wind.

ground line

ORANGE SNEEZEWEED
Helenium Hoopesii

Other names: Owl claws, Hoopes sneezeweed, sunflower, western sneezeweed, yellow weed.

Flower: Orange-yellow and sunflower-like; June to September.

Description: This plant grows up to 1 m (3 ft) tall and may be composed of one to several stems. The stems are fuzzy when young but become smooth, ribbed, stout, and leafy as the plant matures. Flower heads are solitary and grow up to 7.5 cm (3 in) across on long, leafless, woolly stalks. Leaves are lance shaped, thick, strong veined with smooth edges. The lower leaves are spatula shaped with long, tapering bases.

Where found: Orange sneezeweed is often found in moist, well-drained soils on sunny slopes but will thrive in open parks, in mountain meadows, or along streambanks between 2,134 m (7,000 ft) and 3,200 m (10,000 ft) in elevation.

The flowers have an unpleasant odor that may cause some people to sneeze. They can be used to prepare a muted yellow dye for coloring yarn. The Navajos made chewing gum from the roots. In isolated mountain areas of the Southwest, ground-up roots are applied to the chest and shoulders to relieve pains due to colds or pneumonia.

WESTERN WALLFLOWER
Erysimum capitatum

Other names: Coast erysimum.

Flower: Yellow to burnt-orange or maroon; April to September.

Description: The stems of this plant are usually about 45 cm (18 in) in height, topped by a rounded cluster of four petaled flowers. The seed pods are upright and resemble a narrow pea pod. The leaves are narrow with smooth or slightly dentated edges and grow along the entire stem.

Where found: The western wallflower ranges from desert areas up to 2,658 m (12,000 ft) in elevation.

The Zunis reportedly ground the entire plant with water and applied the mixture to the body to prevent sunburn. They also applied it to the forehead and temples to relieve symptoms of heat exposure.

ground line

D. Gafuz '82

INDIAN PAINTBRUSH
Castilleja confusa

Other names: Wyoming painted cup, painted cup, paintbrush.

Flower: Reddish to orange; April to October.

Description: The plant is herbaceous but slightly woody near the base. The stems are hairy, leafy, and erect. The leaves grow alternately on the stem and are attached directly to the stem without a stalk.

Where found: Indian paintbrush is found among grass, in rock outcroppings, along roads, and in open forests up to 3,049 m (10,000 ft) in elevation.

The only colorful part of the plant is the bracts that hide the small greenish flower. The Zuni Indians use the root of this plant in conjunction with various minerals for coloring deerskin black. Spanish New Mexicans use a decoction from Indian paintbrush for the treatment of kidney disorders.

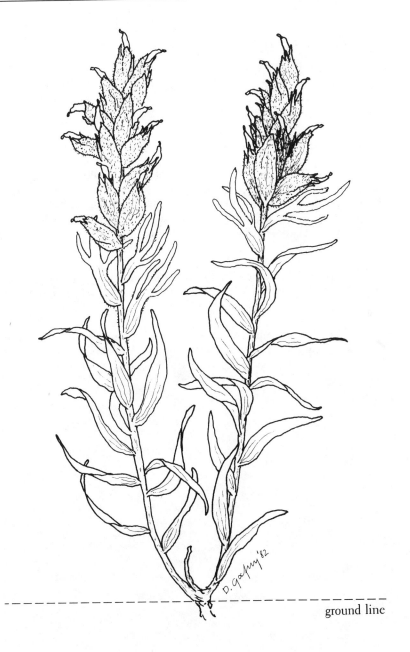

ground line

RED COLUMBINE
Aquilegia triternata

Other names: Rocky Mountain columbine, sitka columbine.

Flower: Red and yellow on same blossom; June to October.

Description: The leaves of this delicate, slim-stemmed plant are divided into three segments, each with a long stalk. Each segment has three leaflets. Each leaflet has three to five clefts on the upper edge. The solitary blossom is showy and moves in the slightest breeze. The five petals grow in two directions—backward or upward into red spurs, and forward and downward into yellow blades.

Where found: The red columbine is found frequently in New Mexico mountains in a variety of soils and locations up to 3,200 m (10,500 ft) in elevation. It can be seen along Sandia Crest.

Columbines are delicate and attractive flowers cultivated in wildflower gardens. Hummingbirds and long-tongued insects harvest the nectar in the spurs. Some bees can get to the nectar by cutting a hole in the tubular spur.

ground line

159

INDIAN PINK
Silene laciniata

Other names: Mexican silene, Mexican campion, catchfly.

Flower: Brilliant cardinal red; July to October.

Description: The stems of this plant are hairy and somewhat sticky, with leaves growing opposite one another along the stem. Flowers may be up to 4 cm (1½ in) across and appear on stalks that seem to grow from the base of the leaves. The petals bend sharply from the flower head, and each petal is divided into four sections.

Where found: This plant is usually found in pine forests from 1,677 m (5,500 ft) to 2,744 m (9,000 ft) in elevation.

The term *pink* is not derived from the color. It is descriptive of the petal shape, which appears to have been cut with pinking shears.

RED PENSTEMON
Penstemon barbatus

Other names: Scarlet penstemon, scarlet bugler, beardlip penstemon, scarlet beardtongue.

Flower: Scarlet-red; June to October.

Description: This perennial plant has leaves that grow opposite one another. Flowers are showy, tubular and two-lipped. The upper lip is two lobed, the lower lip, three lobed. The base of the lower lip, or throat, is usually bearded with yellowish hairs. The flowers appear to come from one side of the stem, which reaches from 60 cm (24 in) to 120 cm (48 in) in height.

Where found: Red penstemon may be found in light, dry, eroded soils or mountain areas to 3,050 m (10,000 ft). It grows from the foothills up to the top of New Mexico's Sandia and Manzano mountains.

In the days before drugstores, a syrup made by boiling the flowers was used to treat whooping cough. It is reported the Zunis chewed the roots and applied them to rabbitsticks (a well-balanced throwing stick used to hunt rabbits) to assure a good hunt.

SCARLET GILIA
Gilia aggregata

Other names: Skyrocket, trumpet phlox, foxfire, red gilia, skunkflower.

Flower: Usually brilliant red but occasionally pink or pale orange; May to September.

Description: The scarlet gilia is a showy wildflower with stems 45 cm (18 in) to 90 cm (36 in) tall, often growing in groups along roads. The flower head is open, and the leaves are divided into narrow segments. The flower may be mistaken for the red penstemon (*P. barbatus*) as both have showy, tubular red flowers. The flower of the red penstemon is two lipped—the upper lip is two-lobed, the lower, three-lobed. The scarlet gilia has five uniform, pointed lobes.

Where found: This flower is found throughout the west and as far north as British Columbia. Near Albuquerque it can be seen throughout the foothills, the sunny slopes, and along roadsides of the ponderosa pine forests up to 2,439 m (8,000 ft) in elevation.

This very showy flower is a favorite of hummingbirds. The Navajos are reported to have dried the flower to be used in treating various stomach ailments. Hopis ground the flowers with meal to be eaten by hunters for good fortune when they set out to hunt antelope, which browse the plant.

6

Other

CONEFLOWER
Ratibida columnaris

Other names: Prairie coneflower, yellow coneflower.

Flower: Yellow but may be purplish-brown; June to October.

Description: The flower has a protruding greenish-brown center with drooping yellow or purplish-brown petals. The stems vary from 30 cm (12 in) to 1 m (3 ft) in height. Leafless flower stems extend above the foliage.

Where found: It grows in grasslands and openings in the pine forests up to 2,287 m (7,500 ft) in elevation. The coneflower is also found along roads where it does not have to compete with native grasses for water.

The coneflower is an unusual plant because it can produce two different colored flowers. The flower is normally yellow but purplish-brown blossoms can appear in the same grouping of plants. The Plains Indians are reported to have dried the flower heads and used them to make tea.

MISTLETOE
Phoradendron spp.

Other names: None.

Flower: Greenish; summer.

Description: Mistletoe is a yellowish-green or light brown dense, brushy growth on the limbs of many trees. The stems are jointed and brittle when dry. The leaves grow opposite one another and the berries are whitish or pinkish.

Where found: It is found along the Rio Grande on the cottonwood trees and the oaks on the foothills. It may occur on other trees.

All mistletoes are parasitic, obtaining nourishment from their host. An overabundance of mistletoe may, in time, kill the tree. Birds feeding on the sticky seeds spread mistletoe to new host trees.

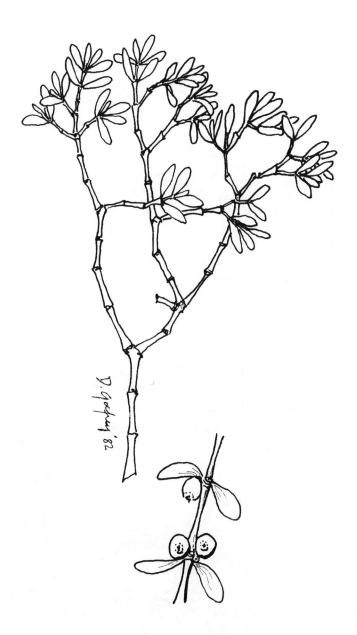

Index of Plant Names